Sell Your Book,
Not Your Soul

Insider Tips for Launching
and Marketing Your Book

Part Guide | Part Planner

Heather N. Wilde

a Hezzie Mae Publication

Sell Your Book,
Not Your Soul

Heather N. Wilde

Other Books by Heather N. Wilde

*Tumbled: A Memoir of Perseverance, Personal Growth &
Magical Transformation*

Pig Tales and Popcorn: Patricia's Memoir

Floyd's Baller, YA Historical Fiction written with Adarryl Hunter

Illustrations by Heather N. Wilde

Precious Child, a children's picture book by Sheri Fox

Dedication

Chani, your gentle, creative soul entered my world at just the right time to sprinkle your magical fairy dust on Hezzie Mae (and this book). Cheers, accolades, and gratitude are coming your way, with the expectation that our delicious co-creating has only just begun.

In Memorial

A beautiful soul, author, and inspiration left us just before this book was released. John Ruhlin was the first entrepreneur I discovered to truly emphasize the importance of relationships in marketing.

Thank you, John, for sharing your unique gift with the world. I was listening...

Introduction

Let's be honest—when you decided to publish a book, did you realize you were also stepping into the role of an entrepreneur? Most of us aren't trained to run a business, especially as authors.

I'm an educator with a creative mind who never thought about target audiences, branding, or sales goals—I just wanted to write my memoir. But as my book was ready to enter the world, I found myself in an unfamiliar territory filled with self-publishing red tape, endless book launch strategies, and a never-ending marketing plan.

This pivot drained much of the joy out of writing. Suddenly, it wasn't just about the story—it was about sales, reviews, algorithms, and profit margins. But here's the thing: when you pour your heart into publishing, you naturally want others to love it as much as you do.

After the initial excitement fades, it can feel like the day after Christmas— you wake up and realize Amazon didn't make you an overnight bestseller, and now you're wondering how to sell more books.

In my venture as a publisher, I noticed many new authors facing the same challenges, often with a "deer-in-the-headlights" look after their book launched, as if asking, "Now what?" As their publisher and guide, I felt a deep responsibility to support them through this next phase. This led me to create a digital guide that started with the basics but quickly became more comprehensive.

Which brings us to this book. I'm not a marketing expert, but a former English educator who left public education to answer a quiet calling to help in a new way.

Many of the skills I honed over my 20 years in education seamlessly transfer to my role as CEO of Hezzie Mae: my English background and essay grading, guiding with a touch of empowerment, listening closely to my authors' needs, staying organized, and thinking on my feet. Coupled with my personal drive for excellence, these qualities have shaped both my company and the creation of this book.

For you, reader and writer, this is the moment to pause, breathe, smile, and acknowledge the incredible accomplishment of becoming a published author.

Launching and marketing a book is a deeply personal journey, and at first, I thought social media **had to** be my main avenue. I couldn't maintain that energy for very long, especially with the results it was producing.

Remember, you're not alone in this journey. Embrace the process with compassion for yourself and trust that your story will reach the hearts of those who need it most. It's also not a sprint. Patience and persistence are both redeemable qualities along your path.

As you continue, let this book guide you, offering encouragement and practical steps to navigate the path ahead. Dive in, and let's discover how to share your creation with the world.

Note About Author Stories

When I decided to write my memoir, I instantly became part of a dynamic, creative community. There's a unique understanding and connection between writers—a sense of kinship and mutual respect for the authoring journey. What's beautiful about this community is the willingness to share and support one another without overshadowing anyone else's creative spark.

My office is home to a growing stack of books written by people with whom I share a personal connection. It's like having a perpetual book party! Each time I glance at that stack, I'm reminded of the magic of this new community I've joined. Not only do I get to share in their journeys and support their success, but I also feel a deep sense of belonging.

Ten authors generously shared their personal experiences with selling their books. Please honor their vulnerability and their willingness to pass down a piece of their journey. While you'll notice a common thread that connects us all, each author has their own special approach that brought them marketing success.

A heartfelt thank you to those who showed up and helped make this possible!

TABLE OF CONTENTS

The Author Journey

Short & Long Term Goals

Wilde Tip #1

Don't Lose Sight of the Beauty

Countless people dream of writing a book, and many even start, but few actually finish. Celebrate the commitment and accomplishment you've achieved—you've earned the title *Author.*

Pondering & Reflecting

Reflecting on your writing journey and creating your book is incredibly valuable. It allows you to revisit the process, embrace the ups and downs, and acknowledge everything you've learned.

Journaling will assist with setting goals and creating a roadmap for the future, which will guide your efforts and keep you on track.

The next few prompts will help you gather the details you need to move forward with your book and shape your marketing strategies. By looking back and setting clear goals, you'll be better prepared for success.

Your Author Journey

What inspired you to write your book? How long did the idea simmer before you took the leap? Reflect on the challenges and triumphs that marked your journey.

Who do you hope it will reach, touch or change? Think about your hopes and dreams for the journey your book will take and the lives it might impact.

What FIVE words do you hope readers use
to describe your book?

How many books do you want to sell at launch? This year? If you fall short, how will that sit with you? Be honest—what sales number would truly make you feel proud and fulfilled?

How will your extroverted or introverted nature impact the way you market your book?

To create the roadmap, you need to understand the destination.

I used to tell my high school students that they could go through life without setting goals or having a vision for their future. Their relieved faces would quickly change when I added, "But you have to be prepared for the results."

There needs to be a balance between going with the flow and having a clear roadmap for where you want to arrive. Selling your book fits right into this conundrum.

Have you thought about the goals you have for your book? What does success mean to you? Here are some prompts to guide your thinking as you map out your plan (if your book is already published, adjust these to reflect on your experience):

- How important is publishing your book to you?
- Do you see your life changing because of your book?
- How significant will the launch be for you, your people, and your community?
- How active do you want to be in marketing your book in the first month, six months, and one year? Beyond?
- What will make you feel successful as an author? What does that look like?

Roadmap Reflection Space

Reflect on your past experiences with selling, whether professionally or just selling cookies every Spring. What strategies worked for you, which didn't, and how did you feel about the process? Are there any particular stories or insights that stand out?

What's your purchasing style? What motivates you to buy, and what marketing approaches push you away? Reflect on the factors that drive your decisions and the ones that deter you.

Imagine creating the perfect store for your book—a real, live storefront! Describe the vibe and atmosphere of this ideal brick-and-mortar shop where your book is showcased. Who are the customers that frequent this store? Are they loyal, repeat buyers?

A Hezzie Mae author envisions the 'coolest store ever' for their book:
"*Hot Tub Mommy* is on sale at a store that feels like an adult version of Claire's Boutique. Like an in-person Etsy store that sells funky knick-knacks, unique stationery and glitter pens, fun nail polish, and different, creative gifts for your best girlfriends. There's a coffee bar, a mimosa station, and a place for pedicures. The energy is vibrant, relaxed, unrushed, and creative.

It's also next door to a cost-free childcare place with expert babysitters and a massive jungle gym to keep the kids occupied." - Nicole Lance

Your Turn...

Imagine your book has three best friends (other books) that it always hangs out with. List your book and the three other books that would belong together. Seeing your book alongside its 'friends' can reveal surprising connections and shared spaces.

Sell Your Book, Not Your Soul's **Book Besties:**

1. *Quiet Marketing* by Danielle Gardner
2. *Giftology* by John Ruhlin
3. *Generating Business Referrals Without Asking* by Stacey Brown Randall

Light Business Sense

Wilde Tip #2

Clear the Clutter

Feeling overwhelmed? Don't underestimate the power of a brain dump. Get your ideas on paper, then organize, categorize, and strategize. Clarity begins with taking that first step.

Common Entrepreneur Language

Brand

A business brand is a company's unique identity, including its name, logo, and reputation, which makes it recognizable and trusted by customers.

By becoming an author, you are creating a brand (regardless of if you have an actual business) Consider:

- Your name or the name readers recognize
- Writing style and the unique way you write
- The visuals of your content, such as book covers or website
- Your public persona of how you interact with readers
- Reputation and trust through the quality of work you produce

Target Audience

A target audience is the specific group of people most likely to buy your book. Knowing your target audience ensures your marketing efforts are effective and reach the right readers.

Royalties

Royalties are the percentage of sales that authors earn of each book sold after print cost. This percentage is called the royalty rate. Traditionally, author royalty rate is shared with the print-on-demand companies for their marketing and distribution on your behalf.

Marketing Plan

A marketing plan is a detailed strategy for promoting and selling a product or service. A good marketing plan helps an author reach more readers and sell more books.

For an author, a marketing plan is essential because it helps:

- Increase visibility to ensure your book reaches potential readers
- Helps you identify the target (best) audience for your book
- Requires authors to outline how to use social media, book signings, and any other methods to promote their book (lucky for you, this book is full of ideas!)
- Helps you set a budget to best use your available resources for advertising
- Sets sales goals with the ways to achieve them

Profit Margins

Profit margins in the book industry are the money left over from selling a book after covering its production, distribution, and marketing costs.

Sample Profit Margin - Amazon KDP Book Sale

Selling Price: $17 per book
Print Cost: $5 per book
Amazon's Royalty Split: Amazon keeps 40% of the profit

Calculation:

Gross Profit per Book: Selling Price - Print Cost
- Gross Profit = $20 - $5 = $12

Amazon's Share of Gross Profit: Amazon takes 40% of the $12 gross profit
- Amazon's Share = $0.4 \times \$12 = \$4.80$

Author's Share of Gross Profit: The remaining 60% of the gross profit goes to the author
- Author's Share = $0.6 \times \$12 = \$7.20$

Profit Margin:

Profit Margin = Author's Share\Selling Price x 100%

Summary:

For each book sold for $17 on Amazon KDP:
- The author earns $7.20 after deducting the print cost and Amazon's share.
- The profit margin, based on the selling price, is approx. 42%.

Visibility

Visibility in book marketing means how easy it is for people to find and notice your book through promotion, availability, and discoverability.

Evergreen

Evergreen marketing refers to creating products like workbooks, study guides, or online courses that stay valuable and relevant long after your book's release.

Print On Demand

Print-on-demand (POD) in publishing means books are printed individually or in small batches as orders come in. It offers a cost-effective solution, especially for niche or self-published authors, by minimizing the financial risks of traditional printing methods.

Return on Investment & Time Invested

ROI (Return on Investment) measures financial profitability relative to investment costs. ROTI (Return on Time Invested) evaluates the productivity and value achieved relative to the time spent on an activity or project.

As an author trying to sell your book, both ROI and ROTI are crucial. They help you gauge the benefits of your marketing activities. When juggling multiple tasks, a quick ROI check can guide your decisions by assessing how much you'll gain versus the time and money spent.

Understanding your ROI and ROTI ensures you avoid getting stuck in activities that yield low impact, allowing you to focus on strategies that offer greater returns.

Here is how I break it down into understandable chunks:

Project	Time Needed	ROI	Notes
Park Point Art Festival Table	LOW – MED (one weekend)	MED	$50 rental Increase visibility High Attendance Quick Sales
Create Bookmarks & Stickers	LOW	LOW	Nice perk for readers Not priority Not money maker
Newsletter & Blog	MED	MED	Helps establish my author brand Increase visibility
Finish Book #2	HIGH	HIGH	Already outlined Improve author credibility MOMENTUM = Sales

Messaging & Brand

For authors without a closely tied brand or business, this might be your first time thinking about how people perceive you or your book. If you're focused on getting your book sold, you're on the right track.

While seeking easier paths is understandable, thoughtful planning and branding concepts can significantly enhance your book's sales. Effective brand messaging and targeting the right audience together form the best formula for success.

Stick with me, and I'll explain why considering your brand messaging as an author is essential.

Brand Messaging is Your Launchpad!

Once you became a published author, people began viewing you differently (including strangers!). Suddenly, your life story, values, and the words you use are under scrutiny.

You are a walking billboard for your book, no matter how niche its content is.

Just as we often buy based on a "gut feeling"—drawn to a book's texture, color, or energy—people are influenced by how you present yourself. How you hold and present yourself to the world can impact whether someone decides to invest in your book.

Without a clear brand message, it might feel like you're shouting into a vast canyon, missing your audience. Some readers are waiting for your book, but you need to get your message in front of them to make the connection.

Who will want to read your book, and who will actually purchase it? They might be the same, but they could also be quite different.

For example, if you wrote a children's book, children might see it on a store shelf, but it's the parents or guardians who will make the purchase. Understanding your target audience involves recognizing not just who benefits from the book but who is in a position to buy it. This distinction can make targeting more complex than it initially seems.

Would you rather focus on getting the child to beg for the book (target audience) or on the grandparent who feels deeply moved by it and wants to share it with their grandchild?

For my memoir, *Tumbled: A Memoir of Perseverance, Personal Growth & Magical Transformation*, the readers who connected most strongly were those who saw parts of themselves in my story of overcoming abusive relationships, codependency, and generational trauma.

I don't market *Tumbled* to a general audience that enjoys memoirs. Instead, I connect with warriors, survivors, black sheep, and those who seek to be seen and validated.

This approach aligns with my brand messaging, where people recognize me and my business as compassionate, determined, and intuitive. I strive to leave the world more joyful and healed than I found it.

My brand message deepened further with my second book, *Pig Tales and Popcorn: Patricia's Memoir*. I was honored to capture Patricia Passero's life story while she was in hospice care, fulfilling her dream of becoming a published author. This experience enriched, healed, and changed my life and reinforced my brand messaging, defining who I want to be known as.

Your Brand Messaging – An Activity

What is the story of your brand? What words do you want readers to use to describe your book?

If you're unsure about your brand messaging, it can be challenging to see the big picture. I use mood boards with my authors to help clarify the essence and energy of their books.

Mood boards can be useful for various aspects of your business, including your brand, book, or book launch celebration.

I'm sharing my mood board for this book as an example. Can you identify the patterns and themes that emerge?

Mood Board Basics

Creating a visual image of your brand's abstract energies is easier with technology than with traditional vision boards, where you cut out pictures from magazines. You can complete this process in one sitting.

A mood board, though simple, can convey a wealth of information. Sometimes, less is more. I create mine using Google Slides, label each slide, and add images with explanations. Once a mood board is complete, I save it and start a new one for different books or events.

I prefer finding the perfect image on Pinterest for each area, while some might use multiple images. My approach is that if you only use one photo, it should be spot-on.

Think abstractly and focus on capturing the essence.

Slides for your Mood Board

Slide 1 - Cover slide with author and book title

Slide 2 - Five words you want readers to use to describe your book

Slide 3 - Your book as a wardrobe

Slide 4 - Your book as a meal

Slide 5 - Your book as a beverage

Slide 6 - Your book as a home

Slide 7 - Book covers you love

Slide 8 - Book interiors you love

Slide 9 - Back cover ideas

Slide 10 - Book designs you don't like

Slide 11 - Your book has been requested at the coolest store ever! Describe that store, its vibe, and what else they sell.

Of course, adjust your vision slideshow in any way that feels right to you!

Sell Your Book, Not Your Soul
Mood Board Sample Slides

Heather N Wilde

Sell Your Book, Not Your Soul Mood Board
June 2024

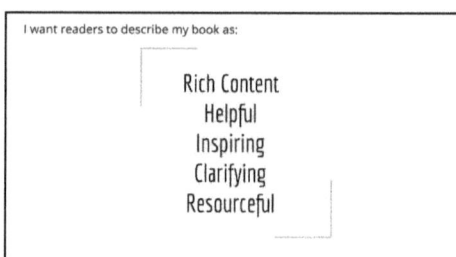

I want readers to describe my book as:

Rich Content
Helpful
Inspiring
Clarifying
Resourceful

My book as a wardrobe...

While we are all aiming for the same goal
(selling our book) everyone's special
marketing style is invaluable.

So few clothes.
So much to wear.

My book as a beverage...

In the end, it's all just lemonade!
Just like all the flavors of
marketing.

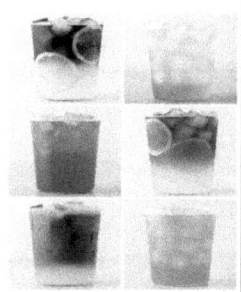

My book as a meal...

Authors need to be reminded
that marketing can feel joyful,
bright, and enjoyable. Add only
your favorites to your plate!

Book Covers I Love...

Minimalism. Reduce the
noise, just like my
marketing practices.

Quality, Distribution & Profitability

Without a doubt, writing and publishing a book is an investment that goes beyond just the financial aspect. That's why it's crucial to carefully consider your distribution and marketing strategies within the larger picture.

We all have a sweet spot for balancing comfort and risk—keep this in mind for your marketing campaign.

- Have you already invested significantly in creating your book?
- How much are you willing to invest in this next phase?
- Do you envision your marketing as a sprint or a marathon?

These decisions begin with how you choose to print and distribute your book, as profitability is key.

I want to share a simplified overview of the three print and distribution options, viewed through a broad lens:

Phase 1
Print-On-Demand
No Up-Front Investment

Phase 2
Print-On-Demand, Self-Distribute
Managed Up-Front Investment

Phase 3
Bypass Print-On-Demand, Use Small Business Print Shop
Self-Distribution for Duration
Most Expensive Up-Front Investment

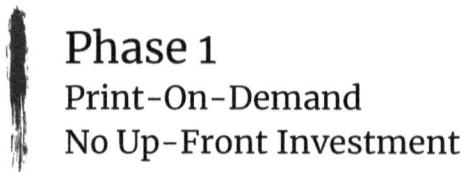

Phase 1
Print-On-Demand
No Up-Front Investment

Print-On-Demand
Quantity Button, Little to No Up-Front Investment

Authors often use print-on-demand services like Amazon KDP, Barnes & Noble, Ingram Spark, and Lulu to avoid upfront costs. These platforms let you publish and make your book available without purchasing copies in advance. Most don't charge for publication.

Value:
- No initial investment required
- Easy to publish and make available to consumers

Drawback:
- Limited quality control; books from the same shipment may vary in color and quality
- Companies take a share of both printing costs and royalties
- You won't know who purchases your book

This option suits authors who prefer a hands-off approach, don't want to invest upfront, and are comfortable with these companies handling the business side while taking a significant cut.

Phase 2
Print-On-Demand, Self-Distribute
Managed Up-Front Investment

Print-On-Demand with More Control

To boost your profitability, consider distributing your books yourself. This involves more effort and time but can be worthwhile.

Plan A: Explore print-on-demand companies to find your book's best quality and pricing. You can order author copies at the print price and keep them in stock. Some companies offer consistent print prices, while others have tiered pricing based on order volume. Whether you stock 10 or 100 books, the goal is to sell directly to readers.

Benefits:
- Quality Control: Better manage shipment quality and avoid issues like damaged books.
- Personalization: Add personal touches, like a thank-you note, to each order.
- Higher Profit: Keep more of the sale price by selling directly.

Considerations:
- Plan your process and packaging in advance, including how you'll handle payments.
- **Mailing Tip**: Utilize cost-effective media mailing services, which can reduce shipping costs to under $5 per book. You might choose to pass some of these costs to your customers.

PHASE 2 BONUS IDEA

Plan B: Manage Distribution Temporarily

If handling distribution feels overwhelming, consider this approach:

In the first 1-2 months, focus on selling your book to people you know—likely 90% of your initial buyers. While every author hopes their book will instantly become a bestseller, most books need time and momentum to build steady sales.

Strategy:
1. Initial Distribution: Distribute your book personally during the initial launch phase when the buzz is high and your audience is familiar.
2. Transition: After the initial sales surge, switch back to a print-on-demand model for ongoing distribution.

Enhance the Experience:
- Personal Touch: Add a special note or gift with each order to make their purchase memorable.
- Alternative to Amazon: Offer a unique experience that encourages readers to buy directly from you instead of through platforms like Amazon.

This approach helps you maximize initial sales and connections while simplifying distribution later.

Phase 3
Bypass Print-On-Demand, Use Small Business Print Shop
Self-Distribution for Duration
Most Expensive Up-Front Investment

Local Print Shops: A Premium Option

For authors who value supporting local businesses and seek high-quality, personalized printing, local print shops offer a unique alternative.

Benefits:
- Personalization: Local shops can provide bespoke features like foil covers or specialty paper, adding a unique touch to your book.
- Quality and Artistry: You get a chance to work closely with artisans who can bring creative visions to life.

Considerations:
- Bulk Orders: To get the best pricing, you'll need to purchase books in bulk.
- Responsibilities: You'll handle storage, marketing, and distribution yourself.

This option suits authors who prioritize exceptional quality and are ready for the added responsibilities.

Balancing Quality, Distribution, and Profits:
Your Strategic Reflections

Organize Your Publishing and Marketing Efforts

If, like me, you thrive on organization, aligning every aspect of publication and marketing is essential for both short-term success and long-term growth. With so many moving parts in book publication, launch, and marketing, having a well-structured system will be one of your most valuable tools.

Create a Master Calendar:
- Visualize Your Timeline: Use a physical calendar or an online tool like Google Calendar.
- Color Coding: Assign a specific color to book-related events for easy identification.

Reverse-Engineer Your Goals:
- Map out your timeline and tasks to ensure you meet your goals efficiently.
- If you plan to launch in six months, set monthly milestones for tasks like finalizing the manuscript and marketing prep. Break these into weekly actions to stay on track.
- To hit 500 sales in three months, start by mapping out your launch plan and getting pre-orders lined up. Keep an eye on your progress with some simple metrics to stay on track.

Stay Organized:
- Track progress and keep your plans on schedule with a clear, comprehensive overview.

What's Next?

You'll find a detailed list of considerations for launching and marketing your book on the following pages. Don't worry if it initially seems overwhelming—staying organized with your calendar will make it manageable.

Let's break it down and tailor a plan for your needs and goals.

Build Your Fanbase: Create a Followers Database

Customer Relationship Management (CRM)

> A CRM serves as a centralized hub for organizing your contacts. It lets you store information about your friends, family, coworkers, readers, and other connections in a single location. Doing so helps clear the clutter and stores valuable information for you to access.

Did you shake hands with a college president at a conference?
Meet someone in line at Costco that gave you their business card?
Discover that your babysitter's mother loves to read?

Record these details in your CRM and forget about them until needed!

Discovering LessAnnoyingCRM was akin to finding a sanctuary for my business mind. At last, I had a designated space to catalog my connections, and the relief was immediate.

With this streamlined platform, I effortlessly navigated through the intricate web of my network. Yet, what truly stood out was the freedom from the burden of having to remember every detail, especially as my network expanded.

I created a special group within my CRM for creatives and authors, former students, friends and family, professionals, collaboration potentials, and even fellow dog lovers (and more!).

You never know when those shared interests and connections might become significant. Organizing them into distinct categories allows me to easily access and leverage these connections when needed.

LessAnnoyingCRM has not only streamlined my processes but has also fostered a deeper understanding of the interconnectedness within my professional realm.

There are many customer management systems available. Please research thoroughly to find one that works best for you.

Your Book Can Be the Heart of Your Brand and Business

Many marketing experts talk about creating a funnel system, where a low-cost or free offer draws people in, and as they get to know "you," they're more willing to invest in bigger, pricier offerings.

It's a natural way to build trust and how I often engage with service-driven businesses.

Whether your book is the centerpiece of your business or part of something larger, don't underestimate the credibility it brings to your brand.

If your book is your main focus, imagine the doors that could open as your readers crave more of what you have to offer (check out the "Other Money Makers" chapter for more on this).

While the funnel concept makes sense on paper, I found myself getting stuck by overthinking it. I was forcing the creation of services and products to fit the funnel model, but forcing isn't flow.

I wasted a lot of time on ideas that didn't feel authentic. So, I learned to hold the funnel concept loosely and let my creative side lead the way.

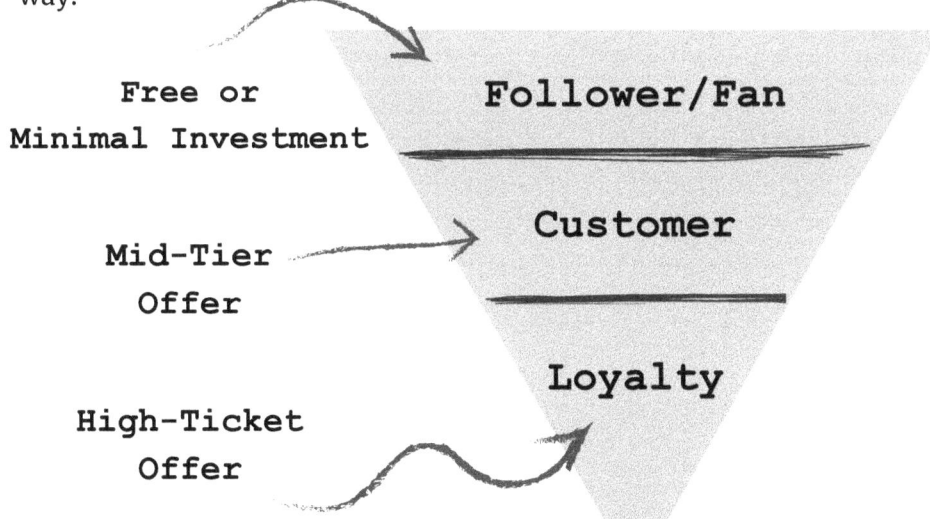

Identify Your Marketing Personality

As you'll soon discover in the upcoming chapters, many methods and strategies exist for launching and marketing your book. Recently, I was introduced to M. Shannon Hernandez and Amy Hager of Joyful Business Revolution. Their dynamic enterprise emphasizes that business (and life) can and should be joyful. They offer a program designed to help you determine the best marketing mode for you.

I stumbled through a few methods before finding what truly works for me. I tried mimicking social media video experts, but the videos didn't capture my brand's true energy. Then, I ventured into blogging, believing my wordsmithing skills would shine. However, blogging felt too similar to my existing work, and the joy factor just wasn't there. I've now discovered that my voice, with its unique personality, resonates best. This new approach is becoming a key part of my marketing strategy, and I look forward to learning more and adjusting my prior efforts to align.

As you explore the launch and marketing suggestions in the following pages, reflect on which delivery method brings you the most joy and the least dread.

The Joyful Business Revolution suggests these five areas to consider for your marketing personality:

Audio
Video
Written
Visual
In-person/Live

Their contact information is at the end of the book, where you will find more information about their programs and offerings.

Visibility & Markting
101

Wilde Tip #3

Don't Cut Corners

Writing your manuscript, preparing it for publication, publishing, and marketing are all invaluable steps that deserve dedicated attention. Take pride in each step, invest the time and effort now, and you'll reap the rewards for years to come.

Becoming Discoverable

Whether introverted or extroverted, generating excitement about your book is essential—unless you're satisfied with selling it within your close circle.

Becoming discoverable means making yourself and your work more visible and accessible to potential readers. It's like putting up a signpost that says, *"Hey, I'm here, and I've got something great to share!"*

Being discoverable is valuable because it helps you connect with people who might be interested in your writing but have yet to find you.

Think of it this way: if you write a book but nobody knows about it, how will they ever have the chance to read it? By increasing your discoverability, you're increasing the chances of finding your work by the right audience.

Now, hold on, Wilde!

What if I'm introverted, and the thought of making myself visible makes me tremble? If I don't want to be on camera or stand on stage, am I doomed never to sell books?

Here's the truth: visibility can be achieved in many different ways, and it doesn't have to push you out of your comfort zone. There are plenty of behind-the-scenes strategies to get your book out there. The key is to find the ones that feel right for you and make them the cornerstone of your marketing plan.

Whether through online communities, guest blogging, attending events, direct mail, or optimizing your online presence, each effort to become more discoverable brings you one step closer to reaching readers who will love your writing.

So, embrace the journey of becoming discoverable—it's a valuable step toward sharing your stories with the world.

Identifying Your Perfect Customer

To develop the most effective marketing plan for your book, it's crucial to identify your "*perfect customer*." Until now, the focus has been on your journey as an author, but it's time to shift your perspective and consider who will want to buy your book.

Dive deep into understanding your ideal reader. What makes them unique? What are their interests and habits? Where do they spend their time? What is important to them at this stage in their life?

Find Your Marketing Joy: *Hell Yes* or *Hell No*?

Not all marketing strategies are created equal, as your book and your journey are unique. You wrote your book to entertain, inspire, teach, or create, and that joy should continue post-publishing.

Consider your perfect customer and how to position your book for them. Explore these marketing tools designed to enhance your visibility.

Don't be afraid to categorize each suggestion as a *Hell Yes* or a *Hell No*!

How does each one feel initially? If email marketing doesn't excite you, you'll know right away—perhaps even feel a strong aversion (like I did).

On the other hand, if author interviews on podcasts make you smile from ear to ear, that's a *Hell Yes*!

Pay special attention to the ones that land in the muddy middle. When starting out, if a strategy doesn't spark joy, count it as a *Hell No* for now. You can always revisit it later.

Without overthinking, on the next page, mark the strategies that feel right and don't produce dread. Star your *Hell Yes* opportunities and commit to starting with only these.

Your initial instincts will guide you to the visibility tools that best suit your book and personal style.

How Does My Book Want to Show Up?

Scan the suggestions below and check the ones that sound appealing to investigate further.

- ☐ Author Interviews on Podcasts or Radio

- ☐ Press Releases to Newspapers and Media Outlets

- ☐ Readings or Author Q&A at Libraries or Bookstores

- ☐ Street Team of Dedicated Fans

- ☐ Social Media (this has at least 102 subcategories)

- ☐ Book Club Talks

- ☐ Book Launch Events (In-person or Virtual)

- ☐ Fairs, Markets, and Festivals

- ☐ Conferences, Schools, or Community Events

- ☐ Donations & Contest Giveaways

- ☐ Influencer Collaboration for Reviews & Promotions

- ☐ Partner with Local Businesses

- ☐ Email Newsletters or Direct Snail Mail

- ☐ Bookstore or Library Outreach

- ☐ Advertising Campaigns

- ☐ Author Website

Reflect on the aspects of your marketing strategy that energize and excite you. How do these align with your comfort zone? How much of a financial investment and how much time are required from you?

Here are some tailored marketing ideas to consider. Evaluate each idea based on effort, value, and alignment with your personality and author brand.

Establish a Professional Social Media Page: Create a dedicated page on your preferred platform to effectively connect with your target audience.

Design a Teaser Banner: Craft an eye-catching banner for your social media to tease your upcoming book and generate interest among followers.

Choose an Engaging Hashtag: Select a memorable hashtag like #tumbled or #speakingtruth to boost visibility and engagement on social media.

Craft a Compelling Call to Action: Encourage visitors to like your page and sign up for updates or newsletters about your book launch and future news.

Utilize Cover Images: Create visually appealing cover images for use across platforms, maintaining brand consistency.

Develop a Website Landing Page: Build a landing page with details about you as an author, updates about your book, and future announcements.

Engage with Online Communities: Participate in forums, groups, and communities related to your genre to connect with potential readers and fellow authors.

Guest Blogging: Write posts for popular blogs or websites in your genre to reach new audiences and establish yourself as an authority.

Collaborate with Other Authors: Team up with other authors for joint projects, cross-promotions, or events to expand your reach and introduce your work to new readers.

Here are additional marketing strategies to enhance your book promotion efforts:

Attend Literary Events: Join book fairs, literary festivals, and author signings to network with industry professionals, interact with readers, and showcase your work.

Utilize Book Review Platforms: Submit your book to popular review websites, blogs, and forums to build credibility and attract new readers through positive reviews.

Create Compelling Content: Share engaging content related to your book or writing journey, such as blog posts, articles, videos, or podcasts, to captivate and engage your audience.

Optimize Metadata and Keywords: Ensure your book's title, description, and keywords are optimized for search engines and online retailers to improve visibility and discoverability.

Offer Freebies and Promotions: Provide free chapters, short stories, or other bonus content to attract readers and encourage them to explore your work further.

Build an Email List: Create an email list to keep in touch with your audience and share updates, newsletters, and exclusive content about your latest releases and events.

Leverage Social Media Platforms: Use platforms like Facebook, Twitter, Instagram, and LinkedIn to connect with readers, share updates, and promote your books authentically.

Book Trailer: Consider making a book trailer, even if it's low-budget or quirky, to create a memorable impression and engage potential readers.

Again, always evaluate these ideas based on their alignment with your goals, the effort required, and how well they fit with your author's brand.

Connections with Opportunities

Now is the time to leverage your sphere of influence within your community, regardless of location. Identify individuals in your network who have marketing industry expertise.

Who might be eager to offer you advice, a favor, or a valuable connection?

Focus on those "super-connectors" among your acquaintances—people who seem to know everyone. Engaging with these key individuals can significantly boost your networking efforts and open up valuable opportunities.

Circles & Connections

Reflect on your sphere of influence: the people you know, the communities you're part of, and your online presence. Identify your circles and assess how well you're known within each. Do any of these circles align with your vision of your perfect customer?

Connections & Outreach Strategies to Explore

Email Platforms & Campaigns

What are they, and what are the advantages and disadvantages?

Email platforms are valuable tools for staying in touch with your audience. They allow you to send bulk newsletters or emails efficiently.

Pros of Email Campaigns and Marketing:

- Direct Audience Reach: Email allows for personalized and direct communication with your audience, making it easier to target specific segments.
- Cost-Effective: Compared to other forms of marketing, email campaigns are relatively inexpensive and offer a high return on investment (ROI).
- Measurable Results: Email marketing provides clear metrics like open rates, click-through rates, and conversion rates, enabling easy tracking of success.
- Automation: You can automate email campaigns, saving time and allowing for timely, consistent communication with your audience.

Cons of Email Campaigns and Marketing:

- Deliverability Issues: Emails may end up in spam folders, reducing visibility and effectiveness.
- Content Overload: Audiences receive numerous emails daily, making it challenging to stand out and capture attention.
- Unsubscribes: Poorly executed campaigns can lead to high unsubscribe rates, reducing your audience base.
- Dependency on Email Lists: Campaign success depends heavily on the quality and size of your email list, which requires ongoing maintenance and growth efforts.

I've found that Flodesk aligns perfectly with the vibe I want to convey for my brand. Additionally, I've utilized the email campaign feature integrated into my Squarespace website.

Side Note: As an entrepreneur and author, I've discovered that newsletters and email campaigns don't bring me joy. Consequently, I use these methods minimally, but you don't have to take my word for it. Fortunately, many resources and professionals can teach you the essentials or handle it for you!

Social Media Marketing

In today's publishing world, social media is essential for authors, offering a way to reach readers globally. However, it can be overwhelming due to the noise and self-promotion on platforms like Facebook, Instagram, TikTok, and Twitter.

First and foremost, understand that you cannot do them all!

Personally, I found it challenging to invest time in creating meaningful content while trying not to fixate on likes and engagement. While these metrics are the goal, I didn't become an author and entrepreneur to be bogged down by social media statistics.

Dealing with spammers, hackers, and trolls added to the frustration (I am meeting with a cybersecurity tech today for some repair work).

After nearly two years, I realized social media marketing needed a lesser role in my strategy. I didn't abandon it entirely, but until I can hand over complete control to a social media manager (manifestation hint!), I'm now comfortable with the level of content I share.

I found that within this chaos lies an opportunity for balance. Social media provides a FREE platform to expand your reach and connect with a broader audience, which shouldn't be ignored.

By staying genuine and making meaningful connections, you can use these tools to enhance visibility and build relationships in the literary world.

Embrace social media in a way that feels authentic to you, whether that means posting sparingly or exploring other avenues like blogging on your website.

Tip: Your posts should be visually consistent and appealing to attract your audience. If designing isn't your strength, hire a graphic designer to create a set of templates for you. Easy button!

Reflect on how social media fits into your life and business. Which platforms do you enjoy most, and do they match where your ideal customers are most active?

Social Media Post Ideas (or BLOG!)

- Create a video discussing the inspiration behind your book and why you're writing it.
- Share a countdown featuring authors who have inspired you, including their book covers, quotes, and memorable characters.
- Provide a behind-the-scenes glimpse into your writing process with a video.
- Offer insights into the author's experience by sharing what it's like to be an author.
- Reflect on childhood books or memories that have influenced your journey to becoming an author.
- Promote books written by friends and fellow authors.
- Engage your audience by asking for photos of people holding books that have changed their lives.
- Share a list of keywords that encapsulate the essence of your book.
- Discuss commonalities between yourself and your readers, providing talking points for conversation.
- Tease your audience with a sample of your book.
- Excite your followers with a title and cover reveal.
- Share a sneak peek of the interior layout of your book.
- Provide recommendations for your current reads to connect with your audience.
- Host a Facebook Live Q&A session about your book.
- Engage with other posts or books that share your themes.
- Research relevant hashtags and incorporate them into your posts.
- Read and comment on other authors' blogs to build connections within the writing community.
- Share impactful quotes from your book to generate interest.
- Include a link to your website or book in your email signature.
- Go live on social media when your author copies arrive in the mail, capturing the excitement of holding your book for the first time.
- Spark discussion by casting actors who would portray the characters in your book.

Social Media Inspiration

Book Sales Sheet

A book sales sheet is a key marketing tool that highlights what makes your book special to potential buyers like bookstores, librarians, and other relevant groups.

It gives a quick rundown with essential details such as the title, synopsis, author bio, and any reviews or endorsements.

The real value of the sales sheet is how it helps you showcase your book's potential and grab the decision-maker's attention. It's a handy asset for promoting your work, pitching to retailers, and even for those spontaneous moments when you want to leave a copy at your local grocery store!

Essentials for a Winning Book & Author Sales Sheet

Book Title: Display the title prominently at the top of the sheet.

Author Name: Include the author's name, ideally near the book title.

Book Cover: Feature a high-resolution image of the book cover to visually represent the book.

Synopsis: Provide a summary highlighting the book's genre, main themes, and key selling points.

Author Bio: Include a concise biography of the author, emphasizing relevant credentials, previous works, and any awards or accolades.

Key Features: List unique elements that make the book stand out, such as illustrations, multimedia content, or notable endorsements.

Target Audience: Define the primary audience, including age range, interests, and demographics.

Reviews/Testimonials: To build credibility, add positive reviews or testimonials from readers, reviewers, or industry professionals.

Sales Information: Provide details on the book's format (e.g., hardcover, paperback, e-book), ISBN, retail price, and availability through distributors or wholesalers.

Contact Information: Include contact details for the author or publisher, such as website, email address, and social media handles for easy inquiries or orders.

Additional Resources: Optionally, include information on extra resources like discussion guides, author interviews, or book club materials.

Call to Action: Include a clear call to action, encouraging bookstores, librarians, or literary agents to request review copies, place orders, or schedule author events.

Visual Appeal: Design the sales sheet with engaging graphics, fonts, and layouts to capture attention and enhance readability.

Branding: Ensure consistent branding with the book cover design and other promotional materials to reinforce recognition and brand identity.

Elevator Pitch | Author Bio

I often stumbled when trying to explain who I am and why I wrote my book, even though it should be straightforward. A business coach suggested crafting an elevator pitch—a 20-30-second introduction designed to quickly and effectively convey your book's essence to a stranger in an elevator.

Think about your elevator pitch carefully. Be ready to explain why you wrote the book and what it's about.

Additionally, having an author bio in your toolkit is essential.

People frequently ask for a brief paragraph about you and your journey. It's helpful to have at least one author bio ready, but also prepare a few variations with different tones to suit various audiences.

Wilde Elevator Pitch and Author Bio

Elevator Pitch

I help people tell the truth of their story—fully and without apology. Fierce enough to name it. Gentle enough to heal it. That's the work.

Author Bio

Heather N. Wilde is an author, publisher, and artist — and the founder of Hezzie Mae, a creative studio devoted to honoring untold stories.

She is the author of *Tumbled: A Memoir of Perseverance, Personal Growth & Magical Transformation* and the YA historical fiction novel *Floyd's Baller*, along with other works centered on courage, voice, and ownership.

Through publishing, a monthly art club, and relational projects like *Care, Sent*, her work lives at the intersection of beauty and restoration — helping people feel seen, heard, and empowered in their own narratives.

Elevator Pitch | Author Bio

Podcasts & Blogs

Podcasters are always on the lookout for interesting guests, and it's easy to find opportunities with free platforms. By signing up for updates, you can discover podcasts that align with your message and network globally with minimal effort.

The same goes for bloggers—offer to be a guest and add value to their blog!

Don't forget to share the episode on your social media and website to maximize exposure.

> Tip:
> Create a document summarizing your story that you can easily cut and paste into their online applications. Include your author bio. If you are multi-passionate, it is a good idea to have more than one bio ready to capture the attention of that podcaster.

Here are seven common podcast application questions you might encounter:

1. What is the title of your book, and a brief description of it?
2. What is your background and expertise related to the topic of your book?
3. Why would you be a great guest for our podcast?
4. What unique insights or value can you offer to our listeners?
5. Do you have any previous media or podcast appearances? If so, please provide links.
6. What are your main talking points or key messages you'd like to discuss on the podcast?
7. How do you engage with your audience or promote your book?

Free Podcast Services: RadioGuestList.com | PodcastGuests.com

Top Donation Opportunities to Consider

Donating books is a cost-effective way to gain visibility and contribute positively. It helps build goodwill, spreads your message, and supports communities while offering exposure for your book.

Local or surrounding libraries	Book fairs and literary festivals
Freebie for VIP bags	Charity organizations
Fundraiser or silent auction	Prisons and juvenile detention centers
Free Little Libraries	Youth clubs and after-school programs
Coffee shops	Women's shelters
Community centers	Local bookstores (for promotional
Schools	giveaways)
Homeless shelters	Airports and train stations
Hospitals	Hotel lobbies
Book Clubs	Waiting rooms (doctor's offices, car
Senior Centers	repair shops, etc.)

The Story of the World Travelor

When my memoir, *Tumbled*, launched, it was a joy to see readers enjoying it in various places—at home, on airplanes, or while on vacation. In the early months, I gave away free copies to friends and acquaintances, encouraging them to take the book on their adventures and leave it in public places.

Tumbled ended up traveling the world, often finding its way into Free Little Libraries or being casually left for someone to discover. One of my favorite moments was seeing a photo of my book resting on a picnic table outside a brewery on the other side of the country. It's amazing how thinking outside the box can help you connect with potential readers in unexpected ways!

Other Money Makers

Wilde Tip #4

Be In Flow

Let your work and creativity unfold naturally without forcing the process. Trust the journey, and everything will align in its own time. You already know what to do.

Profitable Side Hustles for Authors

There are countless ways to earn money beyond book sales, and the opportunities are vast depending on your interests and strengths. When considering your distribution strategies, think about how you'll reach out to those who buy your book—say 500 people. How will you let them know about special offers or your next book?

During the initial phase of printing and distribution, only your print-on-demand company has access to buyer information, and they typically don't share it. This makes having your own email or mailing list essential. It provides direct access to individuals already interested in your brand and products. If you manage distribution, you can collect buyers' contact information and inform them about your latest offers and releases.

Here are some strategies to consider, though this list is not exhaustive:

Merchandise: Create merchandise inspired by your book, such as t-shirts, mugs, tote bags, or posters featuring quotes, characters, or artwork from your book.

Workshops and Courses: Develop workshops, online courses, or webinars based on themes, lessons, or skills covered in your book. This could include writing workshops, self-improvement courses, or specialized training sessions.

Consulting Services: Offer consulting services related to the expertise or subject matter discussed in your book. For example, if you wrote a book on personal finance, you could offer one-on-one financial coaching sessions.

Speaking Engagements: You can use your expertise as an author to secure speaking engagements at conferences, schools, libraries, or corporate events. You could give presentations on topics related to your book or offer insights into the writing and publishing process.

Book-related Events: Host book signings, readings, or book launch parties. Consider partnering with local businesses or venues to host themed events related to your book's content.

Exclusive Content: Create bonus content or companion materials to accompany your book, such as extended chapters, character profiles, or behind-the-scenes insights. You can offer these as premium content for readers who want to delve deeper into your story.

Writing Services: Offer freelance writing services, such as ghostwriting, editing, or manuscript critiques, leveraging your experience as an author to assist other writers or aspiring authors.

Online Store: Set up a store to sell signed copies of your book and any merchandise or additional products you've created. To attract customers, you could also offer bundle deals or special promotions.

Podcast or YouTube Channel: Start a podcast or YouTube channel where you discuss topics related to your book, interview experts in your field, or share writing tips and advice. Monetize your content through sponsorships, ads, or Patreon subscriptions.

Book-related Services: Offer specialized services related to your book's content, such as guided tours of locations featured in your story, personalized book recommendations, or virtual book club discussions.

By diversifying your income streams and exploring these side hustle opportunities, you can generate additional revenue while promoting your book and engaging with your audience in new and meaningful ways.

Creative Income Ideas

Swag & Merch

Authoring a book is like joining an exclusive club, and celebrating and promoting it is part of the fun! Whether you go all out with swag or keep it simple with bookmarks, you have the creative freedom to engage readers, promote your book, and build a community around it.

Side Note: Be mindful of the effort required to create promotional items, gauge customer interest, and assess profitability and value. It's easy to get caught up in the excitement of these creations and end up with a smaller bank account and a closet full of unsold items. Balance creativity with practicality to ensure your promotional efforts are both effective and efficient.

Bookmarks- Customized with book cover art and quotes.

Postcards- Featuring book cover and release information.

Stickers- With book-related designs or characters.

Buttons/Badges- With book title, logo, or character images.

Magnets- Featuring book cover or notable quotes.

Tote Bags- With book cover art or themed graphics.

Mugs- Printed with book cover art or memorable quotes.

Keychains- With miniature book covers or character charms.

T-shirts- Featuring book cover art or related graphics.

Notebooks/Journals- With book cover or themed designs.

Pens- Branded with book title or author's name.

Patches- Embroidered with book-related imagery.

Phone Cases- Featuring book cover or custom designs.

Canvas Prints- Of book cover or illustrations.

Bookmarks with Tassels - Enhanced with tassels for a premium feel.

Coasters- Featuring book cover art or illustrations.

Temporary Tattoos - With book-related designs.

Mini Posters - Featuring book cover or character art.

Bookplates- Signed by the author for personalization.

Enamel Pins- With book-themed designs or characters.

Recipes - Featuring a recipe from the book, perhaps with beautiful illustrations or photos.

Boost Your Book with Wholesale Merchandise

For authors looking to create merchandise for sale, exploring reliable providers is key to finding high-quality products that resonate with your brand. Here are some avenues to consider:

Online Print-on-Demand Services: Platforms like Printful, Printify, and Redbubble let you design and sell custom merchandise—such as T-shirts, mugs, and tote bags—without managing inventory. They handle production and shipping.

Local Print Shops: Local printers offer custom printing services, including T-shirts, posters, and stickers. They can provide personalized service and more customization options.

E-commerce Platforms: Sites like Etsy, Shopify, and Amazon Merch enable you to set up online stores and sell merchandise directly to readers. Many of these platforms integrate with print-on-demand services for seamless fulfillment.

Trade Shows and Conventions: Attending book fairs, conventions, or industry trade shows can help you connect with vendors who specialize in book-related merchandise.

Social Media and Forums: Engage with fellow authors and creators on platforms like Twitter, Facebook groups, or Reddit's r/selfpublish community for vendor recommendations and insights.

Word of Mouth: Reach out to other authors or creators who have experience with merchandise production to get reliable vendor recommendations.

Local Craft Fairs and Markets: Participating in local craft fairs or markets can help you find artisans and vendors who offer handmade or custom merchandise.

My Top Swag & Merch Ideas

Support local by hiring a designer or artist from your community, or work with a local print shop! This not only boosts your local economy but also fosters personal connections that can enhance your project. Local designers and print shops often provide personalized service and can help bring your vision to life with a unique touch.

Time to Publish

Wilde Tip #5

Don't Jump the Gun

Take your time to set realistic dates, ensuring you're fully prepared before making announcements. Your readers will wait.

Book Launch Strategies

The journey to publishing a book feels monumental.

With the limited guidance I had, I could only envision the publication and celebration of my first book. However, this experience taught me so much, which inspired me to create this guide for Hezzie Mae authors and others seeking direction.

Launching your book is an incredible milestone, but it requires careful planning and intent—something I didn't fully consider with my memoir, *Tumbled.*

There is a certain exciting build-up to a book launch that cannot be replicated. The time you allocate for building excitement around your book is crucial. Your book launch strategy should consider the following:

Special Dates: Choose a launch date that aligns with relevant dates for your book, such as releasing a survival memoir in late September to coincide with Domestic Violence Awareness Month in October.

Upcoming Projects: If you're planning another book soon, time your launch to fit within your overall timeline. If this is your only book, extend your pre-launch marketing efforts to build excitement.

Seasonal Timing: Be mindful of the time of year. Avoid launching mid-December or early January, as these periods are busy, and your book may not get the attention it deserves.

Preorder Value: Evaluate whether a preorder period could benefit your launch. Some authors open preorders a full year in advance to build anticipation and secure early sales.

Advance Reader Copies (ARCs): Decide if you want to distribute ARCs to gather early reviews and endorsements. This can help build credibility and generate buzz before your official launch.

Early Reviews: Consider using early reviews and endorsements to create a "Praise Page" for your book. This can enhance credibility and attract readers right from the start.

Book Launch Strategies

Media Outreach: Leverage the powerful reach of media before your launch. Newspapers, podcasts, radio, and TV can help you connect with large audiences through a single interview.

As a side note, choosing to self-publish means the responsibility to sell your book falls entirely on you. Getting your book onto prominent platforms helps, but merely existing there won't guarantee reader interest.

Remember, your book launch isn't the end; it's just the beginning. Whether you opt for a quick launch to get your book out quickly or spend 3-6 months building hype and setting the stage, align your strategy with your goals. There's no wrong choice—just make sure your approach matches your vision.

Building a Book Launch Team

A book launch team is a group of dedicated individuals who help promote and support your book's release. This team typically includes enthusiastic friends and family, readers, influencers, bloggers, and supporters committed to generating buzz and driving sales for your book. Who are your people?!

Why a Book Launch Team Adds Value:

Increased Visibility: Launch teams can amplify your book's reach through their networks, social media, and blogs, helping you reach a wider audience.

Enhanced Credibility: Having supporters share reviews and endorsements adds credibility and can influence potential readers.

Coordinated Efforts: A launch team can help coordinate and execute various promotional activities, such as social media campaigns, virtual events, and book giveaways, which can be overwhelming for a busy author.

Early Reviews: Team members can provide early reviews and feedback, which is crucial for gaining traction on platforms like Amazon and Goodreads.

Motivation and Support: A launch team provides moral support and encouragement, helping to alleviate the stress and workload associated with a book launch.

Word-of-Mouth Promotion: Personal recommendations from launch team members can drive sales and create organic buzz around your book.

In essence, a book launch team multiplies your promotional efforts, making the launch process smoother and more effective.

Launch Brainstorm

TIP:

Boost your launch by appointing a Launch Team Coordinator! This role manages logistics and team activities, freeing you up to focus on promoting your book. Like a wedding attendant, a coordinator ensures everything runs smoothly, making your launch more efficient and stress-free.

It's Launch Day: Time to Shine!

The big day is finally here—celebrate your hard-earned achievement! Feel proud, confident, and ready to embrace the moment. Publishing a book is rare, and you might not do it again. So, revel in it—you did it!

Here's how to make the most of it:

Schedule Something Special: Whether it's a brunch with family, a spa visit, a bouquet of beautiful blooms, or a celebratory toast, honor the part of yourself that showed up, did the work, and finished!

Activate Your Launch Team: Ask your launch team to flood social media and emails excitedly about your book. Encourage them to post their reviews on Amazon.

Capture and Share: Document the day with photos and videos. Share these moments to engage your audience and celebrate milestones.

Provide Purchase Links: Offer a direct purchase link to make it easy for readers to buy. Avoid making them search for where to buy.

Engage Readers: Encourage readers to snap a photo with their book once it arrives and share their thoughts, reviews, or favorite lines after reading.

Get Creative: If you have friends or family traveling, send them a free book to "plant" in a new location. Have them take a picture of your book in this exotic spot. My book traveled worldwide in the first month, and readers loved seeing its adventures.

Build Your Brand: Gather and organize these memories from your writing journey. They can become valuable assets later for building your author brand.

Book Launch Day

Ordering Books & Processing Payments: A Simple Guide

Your author proof copy should arrive quickly, but the bulk order of your books will take longer. Unlike Amazon Prime, your author copies won't arrive overnight and could take up to two weeks. Plan!

If you ever find yourself in a "book bind" and need books sooner, you can order from Amazon at full price. Just remember, you'll sacrifice some profit for faster delivery.

When your enthusiastic supporters buy directly from you, inform them they'll face longer wait times than ordering from Amazon. While they'll have to be more patient, you'll retain more profit.

Once you've paid for your author copies, any additional profit is yours to keep in any form: credit card, cash, virtual exchange, check, barter, or gift.

For books sold through Amazon, Barnes & Noble, and IngramSpark, royalties are paid monthly with a 60-day delay (sometimes even quarterly). For example, if you sell 100 books in August, you'll receive royalties at the end of October. This delay allows these companies to account for returns before sending you your earnings.

There are various ways to collect payment for your books. Choose the methods that suit you best, and be aware of any associated fees for credit transactions.

Common methods to collect payments for books:

1. Credit/Debit Cards: Accept payments through major credit and debit cards via payment processors like Square, Stripe, or PayPal.
2. PayPal: PayPal is used for online transactions and invoicing and can handle domestic and international payments.
3. Bank Transfers: Offer direct bank transfers for customers who prefer to use something other than online payment systems.
4. Cash: Accept cash payments in person, such as at book signings or events.
5. Checks: Accept personal or business checks for book purchases, though this method may take longer to clear.
6. Mobile Payment Apps: Use mobile payment apps like Venmo or Cash App for convenient, instant transactions.

Book Launch Celebration

A book launch celebration is optional, but you should plan it 4 to 5 weeks after publication. This allows you time to support the book's initial launch, adjust your efforts if needed, and be fully prepared to celebrate the milestone a few weeks later.

Having some form of recognition feels truly rewarding. Whether you opt for an intimate dinner with valued individuals or a more significant public celebration with media coverage, remember—it's your party and should reflect your achievement and style!

From my own experiences and those of others, I've found that a party brings a deep sense of pride and humility once the initial excitement has settled. Guests are eager to celebrate your journey, buy your books, and get them signed.

One of my best decisions was hiring a cinematographer to capture the event. A short, one- or two-minute clip of the party became a cherished memento, brimming with warm memories and a direct reflection of me and my brand.

If you want to see three different book launch celebration clips, visit HezzieMae.com!

Book Launch Celebration

The story of a book launch celebration that goes down in history:

In February 2023, I met Pat, a 74-year-old woman in hospice who had always dreamed of becoming a published author. After just an hour with her, it became clear she had been crafting stories in her mind for years. Pat was a natural storyteller—witty, compassionate, and delightfully goofy. Her energy was infectious.

Our journey began the following day and continued for five months, when I spent hours with her, recording and transcribing her stories from her early years. We shared many laughs and tears throughout the process.

My mission was to help Pat achieve her dream of holding her published book, and we made it. Together, we published *Pig Tales and Popcorn: Patricia's Memoir.*

Patrica wanted nothing more than a grand celebration of the accomplishment. We carefully planned a day to commemorate the book (there are so many stories and emotions I want to be sharing right now, but I am trying to keep it to the book launch celebration).

Pig Tales & Popcorn Launch Celebration

Guest of Honor: Patrica Passero
Book: *Pig Tales & Popcorn: Patricia's Memoir*
Venue: Nursing Home, Outdoors, Tents
Decorations: Flowers, Balloons, Banners
Menu: Homemade Root Beer, Cupcakes & Flavored Gourmet Popcorn
Guests: Residents, Family & Friends. Public Invitation (MANY of Pat's previous students came to honor her!)
Extras: Professional Photographer & Cinematographer

Pat sat outside, greeted, and signed books for three hours straight. She was the star of the show---author extraordinaire.

As a special surprise, the mayor of the City of Superior came and spoke, declaring National Patrica Passero Day on August 8th, 2023.

If you want to witness this magical moment, a one-minute video showcasing Patricia's book launch celebration, complete with the mayor's proclamation speech, is available at HezzieMae.com.

Book Launch Celebration Ideas

- **Themed Launch Party:** Host a party with a theme related to your book's content. Incorporate decor, food, and activities that reflect the book's setting or genre.
- **Author Q&A Session:** Arrange a live Q&A where you discuss your book, answer audience questions, and share behind-the-scenes insights.
- **Interactive Workshops:** Offer workshops or mini-sessions related to the book's themes. For instance, you could have a cooking demo if it's a cookbook.
- **Book Signing and Photo Ops:** Create a special area for book signings and photo opportunities, where guests can take pictures with you and your book.
- **Virtual Launch Event:** Host an online launch party with live streaming, virtual book signings, and interactive elements for those who can't attend in person.
- **Exclusive Previews:** Give attendees exclusive access to excerpts, special content, or behind-the-scenes looks at the book's creation process.
- **Collaborate with Influencers:** Invite local influencers, bloggers, or podcasters to your event to help spread the word and attract more attention.
- **Book Signing Station:** Set up a personalized book signing station where the author can interact with readers, write personalized messages, and take photos. Consider providing unique bookmarks or other memorabilia.
- **Interactive Games or Contests:** Organize fun games or contests related to the book's theme, with prizes like signed copies or themed merchandise.
- **Book Launch Swag:** Provide custom merchandise, such as bookmarks, tote bags, or notebooks, for attendees to take home as mementos.
- **Live Entertainment:** Feature live entertainment, such as music or performances, that complements the mood or theme of your book.

Book Launch Party Considerations

- **Venue Selection:** Choose the best location for your event based on accessibility, size, and ambiance. Consider if it aligns with the theme of your book.
- **Books on Hand:** Schedule your book launch celebration only after your book has officially launched, and make sure you have plenty of copies available. Printing books typically doesn't accommodate rush orders, so plan to avoid running out of stock.
- **Equipment Needs:** Determine if you need a microphone, speakers, or a chair. Ensure all technical requirements are addressed beforehand to facilitate a smooth event.
- **Ambient Music:** Decide if you want to have background music playing. Choose a playlist that complements the event's mood and doesn't overpower conversations.
- **Sales Table Management:** Plan who will manage the sales table and how they will handle payments. Ensure you have a reliable payment system, whether cash, credit card, or mobile payments.
- **Author Signings:** Decide on the format for author signings—formal or informal. Select a comfortable and professional pen or marker for signing books.
- **VIP Guests:** Identify any VIP guests you wish to invite and consider how to recognize them during the event, such as with special invitations, corsages, or a dedicated table.
- **Event Focus:** Clarify the main focus of the event. Is it primarily about selling books, celebrating the author's journey, or a combination of both?
- **Media and News:** List potential news and media sources to invite or inform about your book launch. Consider local newspapers, magazines, or online platforms relevant to your book's genre.
- **Professional Photography/Videography:** Evaluate the benefits of hiring a professional photographer or videographer. Captured moments can be valuable for future marketing and creating lasting memories.
- **Acknowledgments:** Plan if there are individuals or groups you'd like to thank publicly during the event. Prepare a brief speech or acknowledgment to express your gratitude.

Book Launch Celebration Planning

Remember, the key is to make the event enjoyable and memorable for attendees while highlighting the book's uniqueness. Tailor these ideas to fit the book's tone and genre, as well as your preferences and target audience.

After the Launch

Wilde Tip #6

It's Not a Sprint—It's a Marathon

Selling a book is a marathon, not a sprint—success comes from steady, consistent effort over time, not quick wins. Pace yourself, stay committed, and the rewards will follow.

Keeping Momentum Post-Launch

As an indie author and marketer, keeping your book in the spotlight and continually engaging with potential readers is crucial. While authors like Colleen Hoover or Sarah Maas might not need constant promotion, most indie authors must stay active to maintain their book's visibility and drive sales.

One effective approach is to leverage your local network. Reach out to people in your sphere of influence who own storefronts or businesses and see if they'd be open to hosting an author signing or selling your book. This can provide a great opportunity for local exposure and direct interaction with readers.

Another idea is to create a contest related to your book. This can generate excitement and encourage readers to engage with your work in a fun and interactive way.

You might also consider donating copies of your book to relevant organizations or causes. While it may seem like a small expense, it can lead to valuable exposure and positive connections.

Building on this, you could create a webinar or a reader guide that complements your book. Whether you offer this as a free or paid resource, it can provide additional value to your audience and further promote your book's themes.

Additionally, starting a blog or podcast that delves into your book's core content can be a great way to engage with readers and explore the themes more deeply. Speaking to groups about your writing process or the insights from your book can also help you connect with new audiences and share your journey.

Consider updating the cover if you want to refresh your book's appeal. A new design can attract fresh interest and keep your book looking current.

Another sensational way to keep the momentum going is to dive into writing your NEXT BOOK!

Showing Gratitude

Saying "thank you" can make a profound difference!

Just because you've joined the elite ranks of authors doesn't mean you should shift your core values—assuming gratitude was always part of who you are.

For me, relationship-driven marketing is central to my business. I recognize that my success isn't solely my own; it's built on the support and encouragement of others. Expressing my appreciation is a small but meaningful way to acknowledge that.

Staying humble is necessary. I don't want to change because my career has taken a new direction, and more people are paying attention to me.

I've learned that giving is the truest form of receiving. There's nothing more rewarding than honoring those who have been there for me—whether they've offered support, shared their wisdom, provided a shoulder to lean on, or made a purchase.

How do you thank those who have supported your author's journey? Have you had the chance to make someone feel special because of their contributions to your success?

My Top 5 Gratitude "Gifts"

Personalized Notecards
Video Greeting versus Email
Social Media Shout-Outs or Referrals
Personal, Unexpected Gifts
Being Present Every Time We Interact

Be Someone's Diamond

When I discovered Pat Flynn's *Superfans: The Easy Way to Stand Out, Grow Your Tribe, and Build a Successful Business*, I found many insights that deeply resonated with my philosophy on relationships and connection.

Flynn's concept of creating Superfans—people so enthusiastic they'd shout your name from the rooftops to support your mission—struck a chord with me. What hit home was the idea that building these connections was about personal engagement, not just designing a funnel to guide people to the highest ticket offers.

Flynn's advice goes beyond merely showing gratitude; it's about actively nurturing and growing that level of trust through meaningful actions.

Flynn offered a fantastic analogy that I've adapted with my Wilde twist to illustrate the energy of a superfan relationship. Picture three scenarios:

Scenario One: You find a ring on the sidewalk. It's not particularly valuable but could be given to a child for play. How much value does this find hold for you? Will you mention it to your friends?

Scenario Two: You find a beautiful, stylish ring that fits your finger and matches your style. You feel lucky to have found it and understand the original owner might miss it. Will you likely keep or show off this ring?

Scenario Three: You almost trip over a dazzling diamond ring on the sidewalk. It's custom-designed and more valuable than any jewelry you own. You're excited to share this story with everyone you know.

This, my friends, is the diamond effect. You want your superfans to see you, your brand, and your mission as a precious diamond—something so valuable and exciting that they can't wait to share it with others. Now, it's your job to cultivate that level of connection.

Where Your Audience Hangs Out: Find Their Spots

Understanding where your ideal reader hangs out is a game-changer for effective marketing.

It's not just about targeting popular platforms; it's also about finding them in non-traditional spaces.

Look beyond online communities to the public spaces where your target audience hangs out, whether at local coffee shops, yoga studios, community gatherings, or chamber meetings. These are places where your readers might be engaging in their daily lives, and connecting with them there can make your marketing efforts feel more personal and genuine.

By identifying these spots, you can craft strategies that meet your audience in the environments they're already comfortable in. Now, your offering feels like the asset and gift that it is!

Whether you host a book reading at a local café or participate in a community event, being present in these spaces helps you build meaningful relationships and turn casual interactions into loyal readership. Or consider forging a relationship with those leading those spaces.

This approach broadens your reach and makes your marketing feel more authentic and connected, fostering more profound engagement with your ideal readers. It's another marketing easy button.

Unlocking the Power of Networking

Networking is a powerful way to boost visibility, connect, and tap into new markets. Your current sphere is valuable, but you must reach new audiences to grow beyond it.

Post-Covid, virtual networking has opened up fresh avenues to explore. These platforms let you connect with potential readers you might not meet in person, expanding your reach and impact.

I've been pleasantly surprised by how virtual networking groups have helped me build meaningful connections and friendships worldwide! As an entrepreneur, I never imagined these opportunities would be possible. Opening myself up to virtual networking has truly expanded my horizons.

In-person networking groups have been around for ages. If face-to-face interactions work better than online groups, please research to find one that matches your interests and needs.

Networking is all about mutual benefit, so approach it with the mindset of giving and receiving. From my experience, offering more than you take keeps you in good graces and encourages others to recommend my book or publishing services.

Some folks aim to build referral partnerships where both parties understand and benefit from giving and receiving referrals. It's unnecessary, but these partnerships can be a fantastic way to collaborate and add value. It's all about working together to support each other's success.

It pays off big time. Don't just be a taker—focus on how you can support others. The dividends are worth it.

Do you have professionals in your circle who actively network?

Dream 100

For new authors, the Dream 100 strategy is a powerful way to gain visibility and build meaningful connections in the book world. I discovered this approach while launching my first book and searching for ways to stand out. Coined by entrepreneur Chet Holmes in *The Ultimate Sales Machine*, the Dream 100 concept focuses on identifying the top 100 people or places that can significantly enhance your book's visibility and credibility.

Here are FIVE individuals on my Dream 100 list:

Cheryl Strayed, author
Elizabeth Gilbert, author
Michelle Obama, Influencer
Gabby Bernstein, Influencer
Jeannette Walls, author

Just to remind you, the key is to be strategic and intentional in your approach. The Dream 100 list is dynamic and can evolve as your career progresses, so stay flexible and open to refining your strategy based on your experiences and changing objectives.

Crafting my Dream 100 list was a delightfully fun experience. It felt like I was extending invitations for these "famous" individuals to join my celebration, whether through an email or a copy of my book. This process allowed me to reflect on those who have impacted my life or are on a similar journey.

I encourage you to create your Dream 100 list. Identify those you'd like by your side, regardless of their influence or fame. Extend an invitation and welcome them into your circle of celebration. Why not have them join the party?

How-To Create Your Dream 100

Creating a Dream 100 list is a thoughtful and strategic process. Here's a step-by-step guide to help you craft your own:

Define Your Goals: Clarify your goal with your Dream 100 list. This could include gaining visibility, securing endorsements, building partnerships, or expanding your network.

Identify Your Ideal Targets: Determine the key individuals, businesses, or organizations that align with your goals. These could be influencers, potential clients, industry leaders, reviewers, or anyone who can significantly impact your success.

Segment Your List: Divide your Dream 100 list into segments based on common characteristics. For example, create segments for influencers, potential clients, and media outlets. This segmentation will help you tailor your approach to each group.

Personalize Your Outreach Strategy: Customize your messaging to address each segment's specific needs and interests. Think about how you can provide value to them and why they should be interested in connecting with you.

Utilize Multiple Channels: Engage with your Dream 100 targets through various channels such as email, social media, and industry events. Diversifying your approach increases your chances of making a meaningful connection.

Offer Value Upfront: Provide value to your Dream 100 targets before expecting anything in return. Share insights, resources, or support to demonstrate credibility and make your outreach more impactful.

Track and Evaluate: Implement a system to track your interactions and progress with each target. Regularly assess the effectiveness of your outreach efforts and adjust your strategy as needed to ensure continued success.

Dream 100

Relationship-Driven Marketing

As a new author, I initially thought writing and publishing my book was the most challenging part—until I realized it was up to me to make sure my book got noticed. Social media hype wasn't my style, but I knew there had to be another way to share my creativity without getting caught up in the social media grind—and there was!

I first learned about an alternative marketing idea from Danielle Gardner, who wrote the book *Quiet Marketing.* She believes in empowering service-based solopreneurs to adopt a harmonious approach to online business, using a "quiet marketing ecosystem" that attracts aligned clients without relying on a constant social media presence. This allows for a balanced, fulfilling life beyond work.

How beautiful is that?

This approach hits home and feels good for me. It allows me to prioritize earning trust and loyalty over time instead of chasing immediate sales. I refer to my marketing plan as "*relationship-driven marketing.*"

I prioritize genuine connections and meaningful relationships over flashy promotions, focusing on authentic engagement, personal outreach, and strategic collaboration. It feels so much better in my body and utilizes my strengths as a highly sensitive person who strives to form deeper connections with others.

Relationship-driven marketing is ideal for navigating the crowded social media noisescape. Instead of competing for constant attention on social media, authors can cultivate deep connections with readers, fellow authors, and industry peers.

Through a tailored relationship-driven marketing plan, authors can empower themselves and others to embrace their unique identities and navigate the marketing landscape with clarity and confidence. Authors can create a roadmap that resonates with their audience without resorting to inauthentic approaches by aligning strategies with personal goals, visions, and interests.

In essence, this relationship-forward thinking offers a path to success that prioritizes authenticity, connection, and enduring relationships.

Be authentically YOU! Create a marketing strategy that pushes aside your uncertainty and instead believes that building meaningful connections that stand the test of time (finger-pointing at a social media ad) is worth your investment.

Curious about my relationship-focused marketing strategies for Hezzie Mae? Stay tuned—I'll share a glimpse of my personalized marketing plan in the next segment.

Journal:
In what ways can I nurture and maintain long-term relationships with my clients, partners, or supporters?

Journal:
Do you have any professionals who you now recognize as valuing and nurturing their relationship with you? What strategies have they used? How have you felt during these interactions? If such professional relationships are rare for you, why do you think that is?

Wilde's Marketing Plan

Wilde Tip #7

Reach for the Easy Button

Simplify your approach, focus on what matters, and let go of unnecessary complications. They don't give medals for extra struggle.

My Marketing Plan

My marketing plan for Hezzie Mae ties together promoting my authors, their books, and my works. Even though these might seem like separate areas, they all work together to support the brand. By effectively marketing each book, I boost the visibility and credibility of Hezzie Mae as a whole.

Success in one area helps elevate the others, creating a cohesive strategy that drives sustained book sales and positive momentum.

I'm sharing my marketing plan with you for a couple of reasons.

I want to give you an inside look at my marketing plan, which is very much alive and fluid. My company is established but growing, so I'm constantly learning, adjusting, and setting new goals.

Much of my business growth has come from trial and error and countless hours of reading and listening to great business minds. I would gather insights here and then bring them back to my "nest" to contemplate and incorporate into a strategy that truly worked for me.

By sharing my journey, you can learn what did and didn't work for me and why. I'll highlight the successful components and how these elements came together to create an authentic-mine marketing plan.

Decisions I made while developing the marketing strategy for Hezzie Mae:

- What are the core values and authentic aspects of my brand that I want to communicate through my relationship-driven marketing efforts?
- How can I create opportunities for genuine engagement with my audience beyond traditional marketing tactics?
- How can I nurture and maintain long-term relationships with my clients, partners, or supporters?

Relationships, Relationships, Relationships

Before diving into my marketing plan's specifics, it's crucial to understand that my approach is rooted in values and authentic connections. Reflecting on my classroom experience, I realized that fostering relationships—where people feel seen and heard—was key.

This approach wasn't about numbers, statistics, or profits but about building trust and belief.

I decided to bring these same principles from my teaching into my business. I already knew how to connect with people; I just needed to adjust my perspective. It's not about the book or business itself but about who you are and how you want to engage with others (I like this!)

I challenge you to define your core beliefs and let them shape your marketing strategies. Focus on how you want to show up and connect authentically.

Who Are My People?

You've probably heard the saying that "bad publicity is still publicity." While I don't want Hezzie Mae or Heather Wilde associated with negativity, this idea helped me understand the importance of staying memorable.

My goal is to ensure that my brand remains at the top of people's minds so that when someone says, "Have I told you I started my book?" I'm the one they remember.

As with my whole marketing plan, this has adjusted slightly as my company has grown. Even with a creative, abstract mindset, I found value in having some structure to guide my efforts.

I realized that different groups of people needed different types of interactions. To manage this, I created categories (yes, I put people in boxes) to tailor my approach. This allowed me to plan how often to engage, assess time and financial commitments, and define the desired outcomes for each group.

As of today, these are my people:

VIPs
Prospects
Referal Partners
Authors, Artists & Creatives

In addition to my mass mailing list and Dog Lovers group, which I celebrate every August 26th for International Dog Day, I plan to add Mental Health Awareness Month and National Tattoo Day next year—because why not?

Basic Outline of My Marketing Plan

Annual Calendar Planning: I plan a full calendar year to visualize the big picture, set targets, and coordinate activities. This helps me evenly distribute my marketing investments throughout the year.

Main List Growth: I focus on growing my main list (everyone) and keeping them engaged through emails, newsletters, or direct mail postcards, especially at new book launches.

Video Notes: I balance regular emails with video notes to enhance personal connections. A full email inbox gives me anxiety, so sending a video is the least I can do.

Special Dates and Events: I add my VIP's birthdays and Hezzie Mae's author book anniversaries to my master calendar.

VIP Surprises: I schedule four special times each year to honor and surprise my VIPs.

This snapshot outlines my strategy. My detailed plan is in my business binder for quick reference (it's hard to take the teacher out of me).

	Everyone	Creatives & Authors	Prospects	VIPs
JAN	Mass Mailing		Soft Touch #1	
FEB	Postcard Campaign		Soft Touch #2	
MARCH			Soft Touch #3	Note & Gift
APRIL	Mass Email	Nat'l Artist Day	Soft Touch #4	
MAY	Postcard Campaign		Soft Touch #5	Post It Note & Gift

Kick Off with Your VIPs

Not sure where to start with relationship-driven marketing? Begin by listing your Very Important People (VIPs). These are individuals with whom you have a meaningful connection, whether they're acquaintances, friends, or clients.

This powerhouse list is essential for fostering and deepening relationships. What makes them VIPs? It could be their influence, past collaboration, or role as consistent referral partners. These people are special to you, and expressing your gratitude will help strengthen these valuable connections.

Create Your List of VIPs: Identify key individuals with whom you have meaningful connections. If you don't know them well, jot down any relevant facts you do know.

Get Their Address: Ensure you have up-to-date mailing addresses for each VIP.

Mark Important Dates for Them: Use a yearly calendar to note important dates related to them, such as birthdays, anniversaries, or book anniversaries.

Mark Important Dates for Yourself: Identify key dates from your perspective, like seasonal changes. Avoid sending gifts on the holiday (thank you, J Ruhlin).

Plan Special Acknowledgments: Aim for 4-6 opportunities throughout the year to honor your VIPs outside general mass-marketing efforts.

Choose Personal Acknowledgments: Decide on the type of recognition you'll use—notes, gifts, sentimental gestures, voice messages, etc.—that align with your brand, budget, and interests.

Focus on Personal Connection: Ensure these acknowledgments are genuinely invested in them rather than focusing on asking for referrals or selling.

After you set up your VIP group, consider adding other groups based on evolving relationships or opportunities.

Funnel Strategy vs. Superfan Strategy: Building Your Loyal Audience

In the "Light Business Sense" chapter, I introduced the marketing funnel concept—turning followers and fans into customers until they hopefully become referral partners and superfans. The idea is to guide customers through your offering suite, always providing a "next step" to keep them engaged with your brand and business.

I get the logic behind it—I do. It took me a long time (and countless hours of planning) to understand and map out the funnel strategy for my brand and business, but something didn't click.

Then I discovered Pat Flynn's *Superfans: The Easy Way to Stand Out, Grow Your Tribe, and Build a Successful Business.*

My philosophy and brand are about relationships, while the funnel approach felt more product-driven. Flynn's idea to flip the triangle and focus on people rather than just products made all the difference. Now, the emphasis is on my audience's investment in me (and mine in them), not just what I'm offering.

Taking back the responsibility to cultivate genuine connections with my followers and fans felt right. When I made my first list of superfans and thought about how to nurture those relationships, it finally resonated—it felt like a more authentic, relationship-driven approach.

The funnel and Superfans strategies aren't all that different—yet they are. Ultimately, this approach helped me break through the funnel block holding me back.

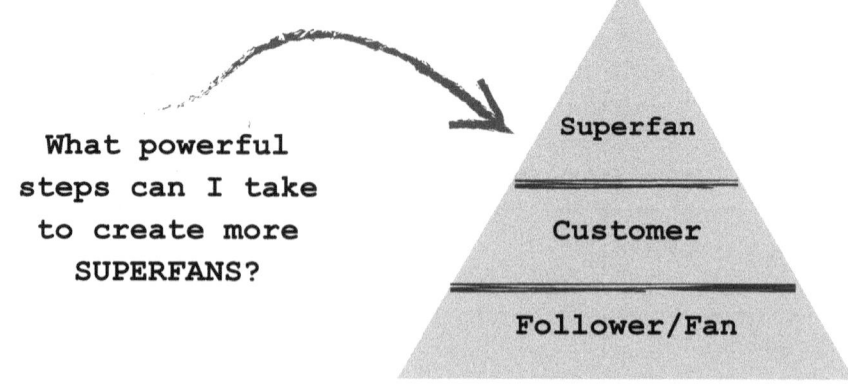

Creating Superfans

My philosophy is that people want to be seen, heard, and validated; here are some specific action steps to consider.

- **Engage Consistently:** Regularly interact with your people in whatever ways resonate with your brand and business. Respond to comments, messages, and emails to build a personal connection.

- **Offer Exclusive Content:** Provide your most loyal followers with exclusive content, such as behind-the-scenes looks, early access to new releases, or special offers that only they can access.

- **Personalize Interactions:** Show appreciation by sending personalized messages, shoutouts, or handwritten notes. Make your people feel valued and seen (this is priceless!)

- **Host Live Events:** Organize virtual or in-person events like Q&A sessions, workshops, or meet-and-greets. These events allow for deeper connections and create memorable experiences.

- **Collaborate with Fans:** Involve your superfans in your creative process by seeking their input on new ideas, asking for feedback, or featuring their content.

- **Share Their Stories:** Highlight your people by sharing their stories or testimonials on your platforms. Show them your brand is about them, too!

- **Provide Value Beyond Products:** Offer valuable content beyond selling, such as educational resources, inspirational messages, or entertainment that resonates with your audience's interests.

- **Celebrate Milestones Together:** Mark special occasions like book anniversaries or personal achievements with your fans, making them feel part of your journey.

- **Ask for Feedback:** Regularly ask your superfans for their opinions on what they want to see next.

My Take on Book Distribution

Earlier in the book, I outlined **Three Phases for Book Distribution**:

No Up-Front Investment: Authors start with minimal financial risk.
Personal Distribution: Moving into managing inventory and more personal distribution efforts.
Full Distribution: Achieving complete control over distribution and sales.

Each phase builds upon the last, providing a clear path from initial distribution to full control.

When I published *Tumbled*, I was so relieved that it was done and overwhelmed by the new publicity and visibility that I focused solely on Amazon KDP. It took me several months to realize how much I lost with each book sale due to Amazon handling the reader connection and shipping.

I soon saw a better way to keep more of the earnings I deserved. I had written the book, after all. I also realized that Amazon alone wouldn't guarantee increased sales. My sphere of influence, combined with time, marketing, and momentum, would drive more sales to people who didn't already know me.

My earnings could have been significantly different if I had handled distribution more strategically during those initial high-volume months.

So, how has my process changed?

First of all, I now keep an inventory of books on hand. It doesn't have to be hundreds, but having copies available allows me to direct people to purchase through my website instead of Amazon. Speaking of Amazon, I'm learning more than I'd like about this giant, and it doesn't always align with my values.

Now, I prioritize making my book available on other platforms, like IngramSpark, rather than treating those platforms as an afterthought. I'm confident it will still reach readers looking for it as I continue to drive traffic to my personal distribution.

A Phased Release Strategy for Maximum Impact

Similarly, you can structure phases for your book's format and release. Instead of launching a hardcover, paperback, and eBook all at once, consider starting with a special edition hardcover with a dust jacket (I use BookBaby).

This exclusive hardcover edition will appeal to your most dedicated supporters. Release the paperback a month later, and consider waiting even longer for the eBook or audiobook.

This phased approach helps build anticipation and allows each format to find its audience. It also allows breathing room to get your ducks in a row, taking publication one step at a time.

Journal Prompt:
Which book formats (hardcover, paperback, eBook, audiobook) do you see for your work, and how could releasing them at different times boost your marketing? Reflect on how each format might appeal to various audiences and keep interest alive.

Reviving the Magic of Direct Mail

When was the last time you received something genuinely delightful in the mail in our technological world? Remember the excitement of catalogs, magazines, *Highlights*, or *Teen*? They were more than just paper—a touch of joy in our daily lives.

Now, much of what arrives is impersonal, like random mailers for chimney cleaning or useless credit card offers The Christmas card has nearly become a relic, a casualty of our sharp pivot to digital communication.

Consider the email-to-mail ratio and open rates of today. How many pieces of snail mail do you receive daily compared to emails? What feelings emerge heading to your mailbox compared to your inbox?

How does direct mail compare in terms of impact and longevity? Physical mail often lasts longer in the home, continuing to be seen and remembered, maybe even displayed on the fridge. How many emails have you done that with?

But beyond metrics, think about the emotional aspect. Direct mail especially with handwritten addresses and the occasional decorative sticker) can make the recipient feel genuinely seen and valued. A thoughtful thank you note or a personalized introduction can create a meaningful connection that digital messages might not achieve.

Have you ever received a package that was so beautifully wrapped or intriguing that you just had to open it, no matter what? It's a powerful reminder of how physical mail can captivate and engage in a way that digital messages often can't.

When a piece of mail stands out—whether through its presentation, personalization, or thoughtfulness behind it—it creates a sense of anticipation and curiosity. This emotional response can make your message unforgettable.

This is the cornerstone of my relationship-driven marketing strategy.

Incorporating direct mail into your marketing strategy isn't just about adding another channel; it's about creating moments that resonate and linger. It's about standing out in a sea of digital noise and ensuring your message is seen and felt (there should be cellos playing right now!).

Journal Prompt:

How might direct mail enhance personal connections and leave a lasting impression on your marketing? How can this approach make your audience feel appreciated? Also, which would you prefer: email, text, or video?

Worthy Direct Mail Tactics

For convenience, I stick to one or two printing companies. I know their processes, save time by not constantly searching, and build stronger relationships as a regular customer.

Here are my primary methods of direct mail:

Postcards

Stickers

Notecards

Flyers

Small Gifts

Artwork

I ensure every piece of direct mail I send has the Hezzie Mae special touch. It's designed to be visually appealing, purposeful, and engaging, making the recipient feel a burst of delight.

Understand that direct mail and gift-giving won't be the most economical way, but this strategy is about making a lasting impression. Sending 250 postcards might only result in a few book sales.

However, it's a long-term strategy to remind your audience that you're a reliable source for products and services.

It's about choosing the marathon over shortcuts. I prefer investing in direct mail, especially after realizing that my email campaign platform would increase to $60/month—an expense I wasn't even happy with!

Direct mail and thoughtful gifts may cost more, but they build genuine connections and set you apart. Invest in these personal touches and see how they transform your impact—are you ready to take the challenge?

Honoring John Ruhlin: The Art of Gift Giving

John Ruhlin came into my life through my first marketing coach, Nedra Rezinas, who saw a shared philosophy between us. Ruhlin's book, *Giftology*, hit me at just the right moment. I needed reassurance that my approach to connecting with people was valid, and that's precisely what I found in his work.

Here's what Ruhlin's teachings have shown me about authentic gift-giving as a business strategy:

Gift-giving from the heart can be incredibly impactful. It's not just about the recipient—it's about showing genuine interest in their life, including their family, pets, career, or hobbies. Handwritten notes add a personal touch that's often overlooked.

Avoid adding your company logo to gifts. Instead, focus on making the recipient feel genuinely appreciated. Express gratitude regularly and deliver gifts in memorable ways. John emphasized the power of surprising people with gifts that stand out rather than settling for the usual holiday fare.

Personalize your gifts to make them resonate. Celebrate milestones or offer support during tough times in a way that genuinely matters —like a book anniversary. Genuine giving is about serving others selflessly, not just checking off a box (and it feels so good!)

Engage personally, like through FaceTime, and space out your gestures to keep yourself top of mind. Listen to what truly matters to others and act on it.

Lastly, weave thoughtful actions into your routine. Show up, create unique experiences, and fix mistakes when they happen.

My Marketing Mix with Social Media

I haven't delved deeply into social media posting, but I want to share my experience with it.

On the positive side, social media allows me to connect easily with people across the state, country, and even the world. Much of my fanbase is on platforms like Facebook, which many people use daily. It's a useful tool for celebrating the achievements of my business, authors, and books, and it comes at no cost.

However, social media isn't exactly my favorite (I wouldn't say we are friends).

The algorithms are complex and frustrating, and I'm not inclined to chase likes or comments. Despite my efforts, my posts often reach only a tiny fraction of my audience and quickly disappear among countless other posts. The space feels crowded and noisy, making it hard to stand out.

Recently, I've faced social media harassment that's been nearly impossible to stop. Finding an actual human to help has been elusive, and consulting professionals has been a slow and frustrating process with limited results. The anonymity people have behind social media makes it feel less genuine, especially when I value authenticity and transparency.

So, I focus on where my audience is, post the essentials, and let other marketing strategies take the lead. To me, that's authentic marketing.

I recognize my resistance to social media marketing and am open to working with a social media manager if I see proven results that justify the effort. That's a future goal.

My Way of Networking

In the early stages of marketing my book and growing my business, my focus was narrowly defined. I was heavily task-oriented, concentrating on creating high-value content, setting up sales funnels, and ensuring that my bills were paid. My perspective was limited to these immediate concerns.

Recently, however, I've experienced a shift. Networking has revealed its incredible value to me. Meeting, chatting, and building relationships with others has brought unexpected benefits. Initially, I felt guilty for scheduling 30-minute calls with people not directly interested in publishing a book.

However, as I engaged in more conversations, I found that these connections were enjoyable and fertile ground for referrals. The friendships and shared values that emerged have broadened my understanding of business and opened up many new opportunities.

Although most of my networking has occurred online, and I haven't yet connected a lot with local groups, these global interactions have been profoundly beneficial.

I acknowledge that I can't do or know everything and give myself grace. I continue to grow my business in a way that aligns with my values and feels right. I recommend the same for you, your brand, your book, and your business.

My Blueprint for Tomorrow

Where am I heading? It can feel like a daunting question, but a deep breath reminds me that the answers are within my reach or already within me.

I've recently embraced a practice of quarterly reflections and planning, which includes tracking book sales and other key metrics. Seeing the numbers and tracking progress over the quarters offers a clear view of what's working and where adjustments might be needed. This approach helps me stay organized and ensures I can celebrate milestones and pivot when necessary.

I'm excited about the reflection and planning period at the end of October 2024. By then, this book will have launched, and we'll have more titles under the Hezzie Mae label. The growth is inspiring, and I want to ensure I savor the journey without getting lost in the details.

Here's a bit more detail on my upcoming goals and action items:

Publish 12 Books by Year-End: Aim to expand the Hezzie Mae author family with at least 12 new titles by the end of 2024.

Website and Brand Update: Revamp the Hezzie Mae website and brand to better serve and highlight the author community, with a targeted completion by September 2024.

Quarterly Digital Zeen: Launch a digital Zeen distributed via email to feature new authors, their books, and exciting updates, ensuring consistent engagement with the community.

Social Media Resource Kit: Develop a templated kit of on-brand social media resources to streamline content creation and posting and learn the basics of automated posting.

Social Media Strategy Review: Reflect on current and future social media strategies to address any concerns and adapt their role in my marketing efforts.

Last Thoughts

The book publishing world has evolved significantly over the past decade, and we're fortunate to be part of this dynamic landscape. With so many new opportunities, being an author is an exciting time.

Navigating this journey can sometimes feel overwhelming, but I hope this guide and planner have helped simplify things for you. I aimed to provide practical tools and insights to cut through the noise and find strategies that resonate with you.

Whether you're just starting or looking to refine your approach, I hope you've found some valuable tips to incorporate into your book marketing strategy.

Remember, this guide is just a brief introduction to the vast galaxy of publishing. There's no single right way to market your book—what matters most is staying true to yourself and your unique voice. Experiment with different approaches, and trust that you'll find what works best for you. The most important thing is to stay authentic and committed to your vision.

Above all, don't forget to celebrate the incredible achievement of becoming a published author. It's a significant milestone, and no one can take that accomplishment away from you. Embrace your success, cherish the journey, and keep pushing forward passionately and confidently.

Congratulations, Creative! Here's to the exciting adventures that lie ahead in your publishing journey.

The Author Journey

Insight from Others

Meet Author Madilynn Powers

The Rise of a Willow

Madilynn Powers is a 16-year-old fantasy author who recently published her debut book, *The Rise Of A Willow*.

She's always felt a deep connection to writing; it defines her. The inspiration for her book came from a vivid dream she had at 14, which she decided to turn into a story.

Despite facing challenges with staying motivated, Madilynn persevered and completed her manuscript.

Marketing has been a new and challenging experience for her. She's drawn inspiration from other authors and used various methods, such as social media posts, interviews, book launch celebrations, and book signings, to promote her work.

Even though marketing is tough, it hasn't dampened her excitement. Madilynn knows that the fact that her book is published is already a considerable achievement and worth celebrating.

Looking ahead, Madilynn is excited to share that she's finished writing her NEXT TWO books and is halfway through the fourth.

Her ultimate dream is to become someone's favorite author.

Her advice for aspiring writers is to take the plunge—pushing through the initial intimidation is worth it in the end. Writing and art are her primary creative outlets, and she encourages everyone to pursue their passions with determination.

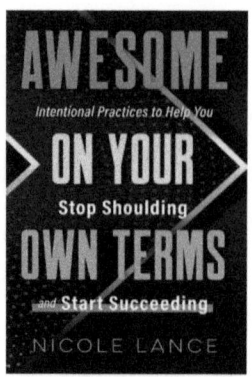

Awesome on Your Own Terms:
Stop Shoulding and Start
Succeeding

Author Nicole Lance, who released *Awesome on Your Own Terms* in 2022 and is set to publish her second book, *Hot Tub Mommy*, has approached the shift from business owner to author with excitement and uncertainty. While her expertise in business operations provided a solid foundation, navigating the world of book publishing and promotion introduced new challenges and skills.

Nicole has explored a variety of marketing strategies, including social media, podcasts, radio, YouTube, and TV interviews, email campaigns, book launch events, and speaking engagements. She particularly enjoys discussing her book on podcasts and feels most at ease in this format, hoping to secure more opportunities behind the microphone.

Another favorite approach is selling her book at conferences, where she often includes a copy for each attendee as part of her keynote package. Her marketing efforts heavily focus on speaking engagements and donating books for raffles and events.

Nicole also values the feedback from her newsletter list, though she finds the direct sales pressure from social media posts less fulfilling.

As she gears up for the release of *Hot Tub Mommy*, Nicole is open to new marketing ideas and strategies and is eager to learn from others and enhance her promotional efforts for her upcoming work.

Meet Author Kitty Coy

Live an Empowered Life NOW!

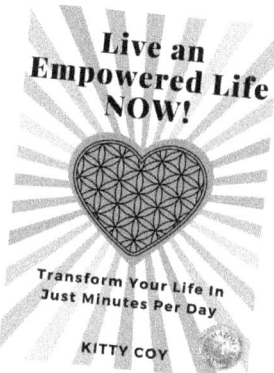

Author Kitty Coy, who wrote the personal development workbook *Live an Empowered Life NOW!*, has had a dynamic and intense journey with marketing her book.

Author Kitty Coy, who wrote Live an *Empowered Life NOW!*, has had a dynamic journey with book marketing. Published 15 months ago, Kitty recently realized that publishing a book is like running a business, a lesson she learned from a Virtual Networkers session.

Initially, her marketing strategy was intense:

- Reached out to friends and colleagues, asking them to share her book or order it on a specific date.
- Attended 21 networking events in 22 days to promote her book.
- Sent emails to over 300 contacts, including those she hadn't spoken to in years.

Her efforts paid off, as her book achieved best-seller status and secured #1 new release spots in five categories. Now, Kitty is looking to re-engage with new strategies from successful authors to keep her book's momentum alive.

She recognizes the need for sustained effort and is eager to learn how others have kept their marketing momentum. With her energetic and passionate approach, Kitty is poised to reignite her book promotion and continue inspiring readers to live empowered lives.

Sheri Fox's journey into book marketing is a mix of excitement and uncertainty. Having recently published her children's picture book *Precious Child*, a story written over 30 years ago, she's now navigating the unfamiliar world of book promotion.

The financial investment in her dream has sparked both anxiety and anticipation. Writing that check was a reminder of the commitment she's made. While marketing feels daunting, Sheri has found immense joy sharing her book with elementary school students. The feedback from young readers has been incredibly rewarding.

Though her school visits haven't focused on sales, Sheri sees the potential to turn these interactions into opportunities for book orders. She hopes to blend the joy of reading with the practical goal of selling her beloved children's books.

She has also made many connections with retailers within her community, where she is gaining visibility and momentum as a local author.

As Sheri embarks on this new chapter, she's eager to connect with more readers and promote her book, guided by her passion for storytelling and determination to succeed.

Meet Author Rachel Gilbertson

Aligned Enchantment:
A 100-Day Reflective Journal

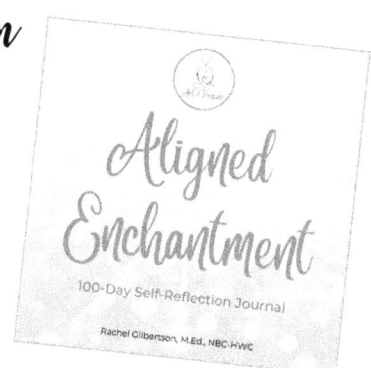

Author Rachel Gilbertson, known for *Aligned Enchantment: 100-Day Self-Reflection Journal*, approaches marketing with integrity and alignment. She trusts her intuition to guide her actions, prioritizing authenticity over traditional methods.

Rachel measures success by the profound impact her book has on readers. Positive feedback, such as readers feeling the love and care in her writing or being moved to tears by her prompts, affirms that she's reaching the right audience.

The joy she feels seeing her book shared and gifted underscores the book's ripple effect of generosity and connection.

Initially, Rachel felt pressured to follow conventional marketing tactics like pushing Amazon sales, but these didn't align with her values. She found that direct sales through in-person interactions and reaching out to local boutiques felt more authentic and sustainable.

A unique element of her strategy is the online private book club she created for *Aligned Enchantment*. Participants share their daily responses to journal prompts, fostering community and connection. Monthly meetings further deepen these bonds, making the book club a supportive and joyful space.

Through these heartfelt efforts, Rachel continues to spread the enchantment of her journal while staying true to her values.

Meet Author Gina Ramsey

Burnt Gloveboxes: Embracing Life When It Goes Up In Flames

Author Gina Ramsey, known for *Burnt Gloveboxes: Embracing Life When It Goes Up In Flames*, has developed a diverse marketing strategy centered on authentic connections.

Key elements of Gina's approach include:

- Engagements: Social media, podcasts, radio, TV interviews, and features in newspapers and magazines.
- Public Events: Library and school events, store speaking gigs, and collaborations with small businesses.
- Outreach: Email campaigns, book launch events, swag, merchandise, maker's markets, and influencer partnerships.

Gina's marketing philosophy is rooted in the "Know, Like, Trust" principle and focuses on personal interactions. Her most successful efforts involve directly engaging her audience through podcasts, book signings, and speaking events.

Moving forward, Gina aims to:

- Secure more paid speaking engagements.
- Produce audiobooks to expand her reach.
- Travel nationwide for book signings.
- Consider hiring a publicist to extend her reach while remaining cost-conscious.

For Gina, marketing is about forging meaningful connections, turning every interaction into an opportunity for personal and professional growth.

Meet Author Jill Celeste

LOUD WOMAN: Goodbye, Inner Good Girl!

Author Jill Celeste, who wrote *LOUD WOMAN: Goodbye, Inner Good Girl!* in 2021, seamlessly integrates her entrepreneurial mindset with her approach to marketing her self-help book.

Understanding that being an author is vital to her business, Jill brings the same strategic approach to book marketing as she does to her other ventures.

Her marketing toolkit is extensive: social media, email campaigns, postcards, flyers, book launch events, library and school visits, store appearances, speaking engagements, collaborations with small businesses, a dedicated launch team, swag, a website, influencer outreach, and even paid reviews from Kirkus, Midwest Book Review, and Reedsy. (WOW!)

Jill's expertise in social media, email, video marketing, and networking has given her a strong foundation for promoting *LOUD WOMAN*. She measures success through book sales and reviews, aiming to expand her visibility and personal brand.

Even as she shifts focus to growing Virtual Networkers, Jill reflects positively on her marketing journey.

Her success highlights the power of integrating personal branding with book marketing, ensuring every effort aligns with her broader business goals.

Meet Author Leilani Austen

Haiku Under a Yellow Sky

Author Leilani Austen, who wrote *Haiku Under a Yellow Sky*, understands that publishing a book means running a business.

Leilani knew she needed to market her book effectively. She started with Facebook, Slack, and Discord but soon realized these efforts weren't enough to drive significant sales.

Recognizing the potential of BookTok, Leilani, who has a natural affinity for TikTok, is now focusing on creating engaging content that connects with urban fantasy fans. She appreciates the convenience of social media for connecting with her audience without the pressure of face-to-face interactions.

As she promotes *Haiku Under a Yellow Sky* and her other Haiku books, Leilani is committed to experimenting and evolving her marketing strategy, leveraging her entrepreneurial mindset to navigate the complexities of book promotion.

Meet Author Inger Kenobi

How Do I Look: The Year I Stopped Shopping

Author Inger Kenobi, known for *How Do I Look: The Year I Stopped Shopping*, has redefined her marketing by prioritizing genuine connections over conventional tactics. She focuses on:

- Authentic Engagement: Building individual relationships with readers, valuing personal connections over broad marketing strategies.
- Targeted Outreach: Sending books to journalists and influencers without expecting returns, which led to surprising opportunities like columns, workshops, and influential endorsements.
- Creative Goals: Using the "WHAT, not HOW" strategy, Inger sets ambitious goals, such as securing magazine features and BBC interviews, and enthusiastically pursues them.

Inger's approach proves authenticity and meaningful interactions can drive successful book marketing.

She is now contemplating launching a book club to further engage with her readers.

Contributing Authors

Gina Ramsey
Burnt Gloveboxes: Embracing Life When It Goes Up in Flames
Humor Essays

Inger D. Kenobi
How Do I Look? The Year I Stopped Shopping
Self-Help & Memoirs

Jill Celeste
Loud Woman: Goodbye, Inner Good Girl!
Women & Business

Kitty Coy
Live an Empowered Life NOW: Transform Your Life in Just Minutes Per Day
Work Life Balance

Leilani Austen
Haiku Under a Blue Sky: Haiku, Silly and Serious
Haiku Poetry

Nicole Lance
Awesome on Your Own Terms: Intentional Practices to Help You Stop Shoulding and Start Succeeding
Work Life Balance

Madilynn Powers
The Rise of a Willow
Coming of Age Fantasy

Rachel Gilbertson
Aligned Enchantment: 100-Day Self-Reflection Journal
Art Therapy & Journal Writing Self-Help

Sheri Fox
Precious Child
Children's Picture Book

Some of these authors have published multiple books.
You are invited to explore their books, brand, and offerings.

Heather N. Wilde
Tumbled: A Memoir of Perseverance, Personal Growth & Magical Transformation
Memoirs, Self-Help & Inner Child

Pig Tales & Popcorn: Patricia's Memoir
Memoirs & Longevity

Floyd's Baller
YA Narrative NonFiction
with Adarryl Hunter

Other Referenced Authors | References

Danielle Gardner
Quiet Marketing: A Calm, Minimal Approach to Business and Online Visibility for Highly Sensitive Solopreneurs

John Ruhlin
Giftology: The Art and Science of Using Gifts to Cut Through the Noise, Increase Referrals, and Strengthen Client Retention

Pat Flynn
Superfans: The Easy Way to Stand Out, Grow Your Tribe, and Build a Successful Business

Stacey Brown Randall
Generating Business Referrals Without Asking: A Simple Five-Step Plan to a Referral Explosion

Chet Holmes
The Ultimate Sales Machine

The Joyful Business Revolution
www.joyfulbusinessrevolution.com

About the Author

Heather N. Wilde

Heather N. Wilde is an indie publisher, writer, speaker, artist, and trauma survivor. She is the author of *Tumbled: A Memoir of Perseverance, Personal Growth & Magical Transformation, Pig Tales* and Popcorn: Patricia's Memoir, and *Sell Your Book, Not Your Soul.* She watercolor-illustrated *Precious Child*, a timeless children's book. She speaks on accountability, personal growth, and recovering from trauma with the potential to lead an extraordinary life.

HezzieMae
with HEATHER N. WILDE

If you have questions or would like to connect:
www.HezzieMae.com | hwilde@HezzieMae.com

Important Dates & Notes

Important Dates & Notes

Important Dates & Notes

Important Dates & Notes

www.ingramcontent.com/pod-product-compliance
Lightning Source LLC
Chambersburg PA
CBHW051317120626
46547CB00015B/2272